THEN AND NOW

Jean Tobin

May your Now be filled with joy!

Jean Tobin

THEN AND NOW

Jean Tobin

ISBN 9798722852427

Published by AudioArcadia.com 2021

Author photo by Jim Tobin
Watercolor illustrations by Jean Tobin

TO THOSE WHO HAVE GONE:

my father and mother
Elmer Hitzke and Helen Lansbach Hitzke
my sister
Marlys Joy Creger

AND TO THOSE WHO REMAIN:

my beloved husband
Jim Tobin
and
Mary Em Kirn   Joe Milicia
Norm and Judy Lasca
Wilson and Charlene Engel

Grateful acknowledgement is made to the following publications, in which some of the poems in this book appeared:

"After Washing Windows I Have My Reward" appeared in *Wisconsin Poets' Calendar: 1992*, Wisconsin Fellowship of Poets, 111.

"Bright Lemon Lilies" first appeared in *Wisconsin Poets' Calendar: 1991*, Wisconsin Fellowship of Poets, 73.

"Dancing Together Across Time" first appeared in *Wisconsin Poets' Calendar: 1987*, Wisconsin Fellowship of Poets, 107.

"Dream of MOMA" first appeared in *Transactions*, vol. 80, 1992, 128.

"Flame" first appeared as "Firewood" in *Wisconsin Poets' Calendar: 1988*, Wisconsin Fellowship of Poets, 108.

"45 x 28, Oil on Canvas" first appeared as "Ironing" in *Intersections: Art and Poetry*, Sheboygan Visual Artists/Mead Public Library Poetry Circle, 2016, 50.

"Manet's *Bar at the Folies Bergère*" first appeared in *Seems* #52, 2018.

"Margaret" appeared in *Wisconsin Poetry*, Wisconsin Academy of Sciences, Arts, and Letters, *Transactions* vol. 79, no. 2, 1991, 234-35.

"Onions" appeared in *Wisconsin Poetry*, Wisconsin Academy of Sciences, Arts, and Letters, *Transactions* vol. 79, no. 2, 1991, 232; *Luce 2001*, 77.

"Professor Rosenthal in the Park" appeared in *Wisconsin Poetry*, Wisconsin Academy of Sciences, Arts, and Letters, *Transactions* vol. 79, no. 2, 1991, 231; *Luce* 2001, 78.

"Tall Yellow Iris" first appeared in *Wisconsin Poets' Calendar: 1993*, Wisconsin Fellowship of Poets, 49.

"The Street" first appeared in *Seems* #52, 2018.

"Tribute to Jim Michael" first appeared in *Intersections: Art and Poetry*, Sheboygan Visual Artists/Mead Public Library Poetry Circle, 2016, 36.

"Villanelle in the Sixth Year of Cross-Country Commuting" appeared in *Wisconsin Poetry*, Wisconsin Academy of Sciences, Arts, and Letters, *Transactions* vol. 79, no. 2, 1991, 233.

CONTENTS

ᛒᛈᛚ

ᛒᛈᛚ

ᛒᛈᛚ

ᛒᛈᛚᛒᛈᛚᛒᛈᛚ

FOREWORD

Despite the emphasis on time in my title—*Then and Now*—the poems in this book are arranged thematically, not chronologically. Occasionally a few appear in the order in which they were written, as in the second sequence which mainly concerns six years my husband Jim and I shared a commuter marriage: he lived in Boston, Massachusetts, and I lived in Black River, a wooded area on Lake Michigan just south of Sheboygan, Wisconsin. Seasonal poems flow, the reader may notice, naturally enough from winter to spring, summer, autumn, and again to winter. But mostly, poems that are roughly related are grouped together. Illustrations separate the groups.

I began writing poems at an early age. Six years old, I was walking home from class one brilliant October afternoon, fresh from the first history lesson I can remember. I had passed the end of the chain-link fence around the schoolyard when I saw two wooly caterpillars on the sidewalk. Reaching down to pick them up, I named them Ferdinand and Isabella, and my first poem arrived:

> When Columbus sailed the ocean
> He never got the notion
> To turn around
> And face the ground
> And never prove the world was round.

I wrote a lot of poems as a child, all others fortunately lost, and a few in college, also gone. As an adult, I found the habit continued, although occasionally.

In the 1980s and 90s, I began to write more frequently, and recently, too, I've been occupied with poems. The poems piled up and, reading them now, I'm startled how anachronisms have gathered. Here are dial and slimline telephones, blotting paper, LED lights newly invented, and my first computer, a KayPro purchased in 1987. Ordinary objects, they were part of daily life—Then.

A word about the Muse poems that begin and end this book. I include them rather diffidently, as two friends who are poets hate them. But I think they're whimsical and a bit funny. My personal muse of the twentieth and twenty-first centuries comes partly from Pop Culture and the myths in Marvel Comic Books. Further, X. J. Kennedy, whom I interviewed for another book, *Creativity and the Poetic Mind*, and who wrote a textbook from which I taught for years, felt it appropriate to invoke the Muse even for the poetry section of his *Literature: An Introduction to Fiction, Poetry, and Drama*. "Give me leave, Muse," Kennedy begins humbly, "I would have brought an epic. Be not vexed/Instead to grace a niggling schoolroom text." In that spirit— although less politely—and having learned what I taught, I include my own poems to and about the Muse at the beginning of my book—and after a considerable journey, at the end as well.

Middle-aged when I wrote my Muse poems, I now, ironically, find I glancingly identify with the old lady who wants to dust and have become the old woman of the cranberry bogs. Of course, I was always the young woman walking carefree on the beach, sandals fastened together and slung from my shoulder. And still, when Lake Michigan is warm enough, I walk, happily barefoot in the waves, along the shore.

Please enjoy the poems.

Jean Tobin
May, 2021

Tree, transparent watercolor and ink

EMPOWERMENT

A fussy old woman in a strange hat
held on by an ivory hatpin,
my muse doesn't like being laughed at.
She looks like she's taking a bus trip to Bountiful,
but she's not benevolent.
No, she's exacting and wants things just so.
She wants to be loved, but distantly—no excess, no bull
breaking porcelain teacups, nothing maudlin.

My muse likes everything
to be disciplined, regular, amazing only
in retrospect. Domestic, tidy, even puttering,
she comes to fuss,
gets a poem written sometimes,
but refuses to stay long.
Shuffling down my walk, politely querulous,
she mutters next time she'll phone me.

Leading her into my study (she wants to dust),
I seize her arm. I am
ready to insist: she'll stay. Now she must
become Supermuse—
a wild woman, strong, powerful, able to soar.
Ripping off her hat and duster, her nylons
and white gloves, her old ladies' shoes,
I shout, "Shazam!"

SUPERMUSE TO THE RESCUE

In her blue-black cape studded with asterisks,
Supermuse soars over criticism
and leaps writers' blocks in a single bound.

Her white tunic glints in the sunlight like a blank page;
her winged sandals strike flint from meteorites
and trail incandescent words across the sky.

Inhaling inspiration with each breath,
Supermuse cradles disabled poets in her arms
and rockets them on inward flights of imagination.

SUPERMUSE AT NIGHT

Supermuse walks into poets' minds while they sleep.
Unbuckling her winged sandals, she
ties them together and hangs them from her shoulder,
carefree as a girl on the beach,
scuffling through sand and poets' dreams.

In early dawn, the quietest of fisherfolk,
Supermuse reels in her lines.

All night, she's searched subterranean depths,
springs of the unconscious, for lurking fish.
She reels them in, hauls them up flapping their tails,
still alive, their eyes bright and seeing,
and lets them go into the small flat pond
of the conscious mind.

There each fish is large, a being
extraordinary, something worth writing about.

Jim in Ireland, transparent watercolor

DANCING TOGETHER ACROSS TIME

Jim dances out of the kitchen
into the living room
in celebration of the season.
Sackbuts are playing
from the stereo, sopranos
take up the melody. Jim's
arms beat the rhythm, fists
clenched. His knees lift
as he prances flatfootedly.
He is all alive with joy.
So I saw my father dance
in the morning to music
of his own making. "What
a fine day," he'd hum
to himself in the dawn.
"What a fine day," he'd sing.
When he'd finished shaving,
he'd come from the bathroom
into the kitchen, and when
he caught sight of me, small, shy,
he'd break into a happy
shuffle, lifting his feet
awkwardly, a man who
couldn't dance, couldn't sing,
dancing joyously to his own
music, "What a fine day!"

FLAME

This winter, I will clang open the iron
lid of our kitchen stove
to place twists of old newspaper
upon scant ashes,
and build frail structures
of bent twigs to enclose them,

to poise against each other sticks
hurled down to slowly dry
by August storms,
and frame an Indian child's teepee
to shelter my anticipated flame.
I will strike a match,

to watch the sudden blaze climb,
and add three firm, clean birch logs.
Then the fire will catch,
to roar up the chimney
in a whoosh of sound
into the wind, and I will be warm,

remembering this October day,
when you felled three dead birches
so they lay just
where you wanted them, measured
out with your chain saw their even lengths,
and stacked them in the shed.

This winter, while cornering winds
scream alarm, and at windows
drifting snow meets icicles halfway,
I will kneel by birch logs,
smell wood chips and October, look up
to see clear skies and your bright smile.

IN BED (THEN)

"Where does the cat sleep,"
you asked,
"when I'm not here?"

"At the bottom,
on the right," I said,
"just as now."

My love,
every night it is the same.
You turn out your light,

cross the thousand miles,
and slip into bed
beside us.

VILLANELLE IN THE SIXTH YEAR OF
CROSS-COUNTRY COMMUTING

I've learned to leave. Now I don't even quiver,
for parting is a practice I pursue.
You live in Boston; I live in Black River.

We used to cry. I'd get cold hands and shiver
at flight time, when they called 542.
I've learned to leave; now I don't even quiver.

You're short on closet space. A wayward giver,
I pack up all I've brought except shampoo.
You live in Boston; I live in Black River.

We wave good-by. A taxi will deliver
my bags and me at Logan. You've things to do.
I've learned to leave now. I don't even quiver.

Take-off is smooth. The Charles is a sliver
of silver light. I read *Northwest Review.*
You live in Boston; I live in Black River.

The lady's tough, I tell myself, so give her
credit (as if I'm split in three, not two).
I've learned to leave now. I don't even quiver.
You live in Boston; I live in Black River.

COUNTDOWN

I measure time according to your time:
arrival and departure. When you drove home
in August, we drank chilled white wine
on grassy dunes, Lake Michigan; gulls shone
stark white in sunlight hottest of the year.
October, you flew home, Flight 49,
8:55, at night. We woke to clear
blue sky, and oaks still green. You'd missed, mistimed,
bright autumn. So did I. In company
of scarlet, umber, orange and gold, I longed
to give you trees. The oaks turned burgundy.
I mailed you leaves. And now, like women wronged,
the leaves are fallen. Brown, sere, they lie.
It's cold November now, as home you fly.

TRANSPARENCIES: A LONG DISTANCE INTO
LONELINESS AND BACK

You know what it is now. Last month
I wandered into your Mom's backyard
after a run, and looking up, you
saw me, standing barefoot on the moss
under the dogwood tree. You left
your mother, cup in hand, and
came out from behind the window
where, you said, you'd spent childhood,
lonely, and adolescence, longing.
I'd walked into that empty space
to stand under the dogwood tree,
trunk thinner then, its new bark
unshaded, and to stand where new moss
would have grown, had there been shade.

Just so, you once walked under trees
where season after season of your absence
I'd watched leaves bud and grow, flame
briefly, and fall. I'd watched trees bloom
in February, with snow, and grow bare
in spring. For months, nothing moved
but green. And then, one morning
as I sat, coffee cup in hand, you
walked across my window view, and stood
under the trees, and I went out to join you.

QUOTIDIAN

We were happy last year in our own way,
you in Boston, me in Black River—
happy in phone calls each night for an hour,
happy in knowing our love. But when that company
says "reach out and touch someone," it's not
the same, let me tell you. Touching their damn
slimline telephone available in sixteen colors
isn't the same as touching your warm, soft side,
isn't like fingering jut and hollow of hipbone,
isn't like snuggling my face in the warm place
under your chin. I could hold the receiver
between my shoulder and my ear and hear
your low voice, but it wasn't the same.
Even though I could look out the window at tall
white pine and watch juncos and blue jays
feast at the feeder, and our bedroom has
no view, the view in our bedroom is better,
when you're there, and I can reach out and
touch, not someone, but you. All last year
I longed for the mundane, longed to take you
for granted, longed to know that when
you telephoned, you were just down the road,
concerned about lunch and the hour and the news
in the morning paper. I longed to look up,
not expecting, and to see your bright hair
and corduroy jacket disappearing up a hill
slowly enough so if I drove fast I could
give you a ride. I longed to meet you
after work and unload my irritations after
you'd unloaded yours. I wanted us
to feel married and forget, until we counted,

how many years. I wanted our travelling to
the airport be to pick up friends, and our
leaving there be together. All last year,
I longed for this extraordinary ordinary year.

IN BED (NOW)

We don't snuggle the way we
used to, my head on your shoulder,
our arms wrapped around each other
all the night through. You have a bad hip; my
right knee is shot. Our joints are stiff.
We spoon loosely now and not long,
yet long enough to feel warmth and
closeness, momentarily skin tight.
We straighten out; each takes a side.
During the night, through the dark, I
sense your arm reaching across space
seeking reassurance, feel
your hand tapping my pillow, my face.
Yes, my darling, we're still
together. Yes, I'm here. I'm still here.

Tranquil Pond, transparent watercolor and ink

MODERN WOMEN:
EIGHT POEMS FROM PAINTINGS

1

Pensive
(James McNeill Whistler's *The Little White Girl*, 1864)

Her face is beautiful, but slightly sad,
her eyes downcast, while gazing at the ring
on a finger of her outstretched hand. She's clad
in ruffled, delicate white, a dress for spring
and charming innocence. Her pale face
in profile against her dark, abundant hair
appears again, above the fireplace—
a double portrait—reflected in the mirror.
Her right hand holds a brightly colored fan.
An oriental vase, red lacquer jar,
azalea in full bloom: such objects can
expose an inner life, roaming afar.
  So Whistler paints his White Girl, his color scheme
  in mostly black and greys, in white and cream.

Manet's *Bar at the Folies Bergère*
(1882)

She stands behind the absinthe, in her frame,
so young, with inward gaze, unworldly air,
a solitary woman with no name,
who works the night shift at Folies Bergère.
Dressed all in black, with neat, white, gauzy lace
at wrist and collar, with an hourglass waist,
she waits alone, with wistful, pensive face.
Behind her, in the crowd, couples embraced
or drinking are reflected in the mirror,
and so are chandeliers, in gauzy light.
Here is a high point in Manet's career:
this patterning of grey and black and white.
    So artless, still, and decorous she seems,
    her lowered eyes so haunted by lost dreams.

Dream of MOMA
(Rousseau's *Yadwiga's Dream*, 1910)

A confounded round-eyed lion looks straight out
the canvas. She, poised calmly, lying nude
upon a jungle divan hears intrude
a black man garbed in rainbow loincloth, doubt-
lessly hears melodies to ravish. His
seductive clarinet beguiles the moon,
now rising round and ghostly, begs full blooms
of heavy-headed lotus, blue and reddish
pink, entreats gold-winged, long birds to listen
to his song on silent canvas. Toward
her lifting high his trunk, an elephant
is hidden in the background—leaves that glisten
brightly, edged in yellow, sharp as swords,
precisely painted from Jardin des Plantes.

Oil on Canvas, 45 x 28
(Picasso's *Woman Ironing*, 1904)

Ah—her weariness is accentuated by the falling line
of her left shoulder. See her lean into her hot iron,
her breast flattened under that curve of body and head.
A bowl for water, a rag for wetting are before her,
the cloth she irons flat upon—perhaps—a table, her
flat iron heavy: iron bottom, wooden handle. These
simple objects are foreground, as is right. To the right
her left shoulder juts up high into the corner
of the canvas. It falls, as does her head, down, her
hair and right arm hanging at the same right angle.
In her room it's dark. Piled clothing waits for her
in the background. Her dress, her arms, are of the same
white daubs she irons. She is her background; she
will never escape the canvas. Always she will iron,
with dark eyes, sensitive lips, delicate hands.

The Brothel
(Picasso's *Demoiselles d'Avignon*, 1907)

Les Demoiselles d'Avignon display
themselves, backs arched with pointed elbows high
and hands behind their heads—five nudes Leger
would paint as if machines. Picasso's way
is subtler. Lost in shape and boredom, they
wear squares of shade for breasts, gauze robes, flat
    planes
to angle sharply at thin waists, thick thighs.
One's framed in flattened, clouded drape of sky.
The brothel's cosmopolitan. Two say
(masked eyes askew, ridged noses curved astray)
they're African. And she's Egyptian,
claims the one in profile stuck with frontal eye.
Both dark-eyed girls are Spanish; this is home:
a Barcelona street called Avignon*.

* *In Barcelona, the street is Calle de Aviñón; Picasso was living
in Paris at the time.*

The Street
(de Chirico's *Melancholy and Mystery of a Street*, 1914)

A girl in shadow runs the lighted street,
herself a shadow in old-fashioned dress.
Rolling a hoop, she runs on stylized feet,
wears pantaloons, a stick, a bow, and tresses
blown back—a nineteenth-century valentine,
stuck in her place. The only movement, wind.

Alarmingly, an arcade dwindles. Lines
severely modern make the scene. We find
de Chirico confused laws of perspective:
each set of arches strictly follows its own.
In distance, human figures grow:
a massive shadow, still and flat, awaits. She is alone.

The street is empty, ochre, but the sky
gleams brilliant green. A red flag flies.

Three Women
(Leger's *Three Women: Le Grand Déjeuner,* 1921)

They sit immobile as machines at rest,
skin like inflated armor to the neck.
Yet, helmets off, now they have met the test,
small heads display fine features, even flecks
of pride in eyes so guarded, stoic, bland—
the new Grande Odalisque, almost, but not,
their challenge done. Rounded, metallic, like shields
before them, breasts and knees protect in field
turned bedroom, yet to passersby must yield
up nudity. The best defense: conceal
with camouflage. On breakfast table, stand
cluttered apples, sugar, toast, coffee, pot
of tea, a spoon. A focal point: bright red,
the table dazzles eyes, obscures the bed.

Mother-in-Law's Tongue, or *Sanserieria trifasciata*
(Grant Wood's *Woman with Plants,* 1929)

The potted plant she holds is sturdy, tough,
long-lasting under harsh conditions. She,
the artist's mother, also lasts—enough
to say she's weathered all. She's old. And see,
how sheaves, windmill, house, fields, and rounded hills
behind her show how well she tends this earth,
her pioneer eyes yet gazing westward still.
Such quiet dignity declares her worth.
Grant's made an honest painting stripped to bare
essentials, like her spare and upright plant
in simple, earthen pot. She's dressed with care
in Sunday black, her cherished jewelry scant,
green apron rickrack-trimmed, her hair smoothed back
neatly, her grey eyes dimmed by cataracts.

CR80CR80

Tamburlaine the Great
Part One
(Christopher Marlowe, 1590)

(Performed by American Players Theatre,
Spring Green, Wisconsin, in the summer of 1983,
their fourth season.)*

Tamburlaine wore his hair blown back, reddish-brown,
light and fine. He rode, strode, swore, seduced men's
       hearts
to follow him, renounce their king and crown,
yield troops up to his cause. In martial arts
most skilled, he won by speech most often. Won
Zenocrate by honeyed words: "Else
you will be slave"—and she, most fearful, stunned
into obedience, submitted, chaste
yet captivated. Tamburlaine encaged
Bajareth, Emperor of Turks, and tossed
raw taunts with scraps from table. Lost,
the Turk turned footstool, fool, and poor enraged
Zabina, Empress, died with him. In vain
did Virgins of Damascus plead, all slain.

* *Randall Duk Kim played Tamburlaine. Lee Elmer Ernst was a Virgin of Damascus. Zenocrate was played by Victoria Constan, Bajareth by Charles Stransky, and Zabina by Andrea Mitchell.*

PICASSO'S *Girl before a Mirror*
(1932)

The woman in the mirror looks out, but does
not catch my eye. The girl at the mirror
is both sun and moon, her silvery profile
placed in a full, round face, glowing yellow.

She regards the woman she will become,
dark and mysterious, mostly ovals, blue and green.
No blue, no green, exist at present in her world,
so warm now, all red and yellow dotted diamonds.

With both hands, she reaches for the mirror,
hangs onto her future. Her arms surround the frame,
but the arms of the woman do not reach back.
Her girl's body shows a womb, round in pear-shaped

belly, empty still, her breasts high and even.
The woman's breasts have slipped, slanting.
Her face is both white profile—chalky, not silvery—
and dark oval, with red and green forehead.

The girl's face is serene, looking forward.
Looking back, the woman's face is not.

TRIBUTE TO JIM MICHAEL
(Phyllis Brillowski's *Follow Your Path*, 2016)

You remember that pink flowering tree or
one very much like it. It was April or May. We
were at the end of Eighth Street maybe,
or on the riverfront, up the hill, looking at that path.
You remember Jim Michael, already old, saying
"You can use 'Opera' here," a bold pink-magenta,
a color—like flowers—perfect, but impermanent,
a tube of paint Jim usually disdained.
We trained with him, meeting at eight
or eight-thirty in the Art Center parking lot,
driving in caravan to paint en plein air.
Dependent on weather, foul or fair, Jim
knew always where to go. He'd do a demo
for beginners, making a landscape breathtaking
in subtle shifts of blues and greens,
in washes of cerulean and permanent rose.
"See, it's just shapes," he'd say, vigorously
brushing in the background trees.
We'd set up our gear—our easels and boards,
our paints and brushes—paint two hours or three,
then gather for critique, munching on
our sandwiches and chips, a prepared lunch,
sitting on lawn chairs we'd tucked into our cars,
watching Jim exclaim generously over our daubs.
You remember this opera-tinted pink tree; we all
saw it, perfect and impermanent, its flowers falling.
You remember Jim Michael—kind and curmudgeonly
          man
with his sense of humor and passion for painting.

Autumn Path, transparent watercolor

MARGARET

"It is Margaret you mourn for."
Gerard Manley Hopkins, "Spring and Fall"

During this last terrible week
odd things happen. She can't hear
for three minutes while jogging, or speak.
She veers left into traffic and can't veer
back. Left and right, she can feel
cars passing, most drivers not slowing.
Meanwhile, her vision, amazingly, blips
hard like film at the end of a reel.
She hangs on, afraid, as consciousness slips
away, eddies, pools at the point of going.

Two days later she is deep within
depression which drowns, is terrifying.
Nothing seems sweet as oblivion.
Mostly she is a fierce drive toward dying.
She recalls three lines from Keats—"in spite of all,
Some shape of beauty moves away the pall
from our dark spirts"—and hangs on, giving
herself flowers to remember how, always, petals
full of light make days worth living.
She tells herself it's not her Self, but chemicals.

For several days, she's lost within a mind,
odd memories gone, fog licking
at edges of words. Like a blind
woman in new territory picking
her way, she stumbles in her individual
dark. She cannot name her street. Only
her fingers remember her phone number

to trace it on the dial. Residual
memories remain like spars of rotted lumber.
Never has she felt so lonely.

Always, she'd hoped the spirit floated free,
rising white, raucous, full
of strident life, lifting up entire from debris,
sturdy as a herring gull.
Once she'd watched an ailing
woman die, and felt the room fill up with grace.
Locked in her capsule now, communication
cut, all systems failing,
she feels herself compacted, a new sensation,
is forced still deeper into smaller space.

WINTER CAFÉ, HARVARD SQUARE

Grasping a metal NO SMOKING sign,
the tall man in white uniform towers
above someone in the corner.

"I'm telling you, you're out of line.
That's enough now," he says, crashing
the sign down in clattering punctuation,

both emphasis and threat.
(Smoking beyond the new boundary,
 a man glances at his cigarette

in small alarm, mentally
rearranges his
rights, and resumes

his reading.) I can hear
but not see the person in the corner.
Mostly, out of tune,

he's been humming along with Bach,
played discreetly above coffee
and croissants. January.

Outside, it's record cold.
Now, the small man, with stringy hair and
unproud beard, very old,

stands up, not straight,
curves himself over his chest, waits
a moment, coughs, waits.

I look through windows, double-paned,
at people puffing empty captions
above their heads. "Aren't you going,"

says the tall man in white uniform,
no question in his level voice.
He turns away. Inside, it's warm.

Reluctant, hurt, the small man lingers,
buttons his flannel shirt
slowly, with shaking fingers,

unsteadily smiles,
stumbles around the potted fig tree,
then wavers down an aisle piled

high, each serviceable chair
covered with mittens, mufflers, coats.
His head and hands are bare.

In full rout, he walks between readers,
each with book and coffee cup.
(No one looks up.) He goes out.

RELATIONSHIPS: DRIFTING RINGS OF SMOKE

Fingers unsteady,
Marie lights a cigarette,
instead
talks.

"My sister,"
says Marie,
"was a difficult woman
by the time she was five."

Pursing red lips, Marie
exhales,
watches
the ring float,
tries again.

"My sister," says Marie,
"was older, wiser, smarter,
more accomplished,
stronger, wirier,
trickier.
She knew how to get me, good.
She played power games
before, in the Sixties,
they wrote those books."

Lazily
a second and third
smoke ring
float
and interlock.

"My sister,"
says Marie,
"knew what she wanted
and what she wanted was
a slave.
And money.
She figured it out early,
love didn't count for much.
Love was stupid.
Lovers could be used."

Drifting apart in the air,
disintegrating
rings
become shredded
smoke.

"What I dislike more about her,"
says Marie,
"is the betrayal I feel,
is the hatred I feel for nobody else,
is the ugliness she brings into my world,
leaving me to wonder if it's only me,
me the one who's been mistaken,
me the one who's betrayed,
me the one who's wrong
and cruel

and needs to become loving,
me who needs to forgive
and be forgiven."

Gently
tattered rags of smoke
move
beyond reach.

"All my life she's been less
a sister," says Marie,
"and more a problem.
She once told me,
still adoring,
still the little sister,
'Just because we're sisters,
doesn't mean we have to be friends.'"

Marie stubs out her cigarette,
unfinished, crudely bent,
marked, it seems, with blood.

"I don't like her now,"
Says Marie.
"I dislike her now.
Such feelings are hard to admit?
I don't trust her.
I can't trust her."

Insubstantial
as drifting smoke,
Marie gets up to leave.

46

"Too often,"
says Marie softly,
"I've lain back in the safety
net of family trust
to find she's busy cutting holes."

ANDREW

1

He sat rocking,
dressed in military
fatigues,
a khaki jacket, camouflage shirt,
loose camouflage pants,
jungle boots,
hiding out in the classroom
deep inside himself,
hiding.

2

He stood quietly, receptive,
head down, ski cap
pulled down, his eyes
invisible, waiting.
He answered questions in a
full voice, ready,
answering only what I
asked, waiting
for me to ask
the right questions,
cooperating
but only so far,
needing me and
willing me,
to ask the right
questions.

He sat rocking
back and forth, back and forth,
while classmates tried
to ignore him, glancing
sideways, smiling in
confusion, they unwanting
to see distress, he
insisting they do so,
moaning as he rocked,
hitting his head, saying,
"I've a block in there;
I'm blocked," and they not
listening, they tuning out,
they not wanting to know
anything about blockage,
about feeling sad,
about waste,
about him.

Pine Shadows, transparent watercolor

THOUGHTS WHILE CONTEMPLATING SNOW MELTING AGAIN JUST BEFORE CHRISTMAS IN SOUTHERN WISCONSIN

In my childhood, snow was trustworthy.
It came in November and lasted past—
although we didn't know it—weeks
magnolias bloomed on Marlborough in Boston.

Ice was durable and permanent.
All winter long I could walk with my friends
down darkened streets
to the blaze of light over the pond,
and skate until closing,
fastest on the rink in my father's old hockey skates,
toes stuffed with extra stockings.

In my childhood,
we could slide down hills in cardboard boxes,
month after month,
while day after day the icy path got
longer, faster
until at last, launching ourselves from the top
of the hill
we melded with snowflakes
and the wind.

All winter long,
snow crunched under our homemade snowshoes,
and deer startled to the sound in that crisp air.

In my childhood,
when we made angels in the snow,
they lasted an eternity.

NEW YEAR

This January cold comes right on cue.
We wake to brilliant sky and five below:
Frost rimes the world. We see on our window
exotic white furled fans and feathers grow.

We walk outside as neighbors hail hello
and shout "A Happy New Year!" We in two
great puffs of whitened breath reply, then go
down to the lake on paths drifted with snow.

We stop to hear one solitary crow
and find deer tracks. Now steaming into low
cloud banks, the water is the deepest blue!
Below the dunes we startle one small doe.

At home, you turn the tree lights on. I sew,
while you make hot mulled wine. The stereo
plays softly Bach's sweet, slow "Adagio"
for strings. We are content. Our year is new.

PEOPLE ARE THROWING OUT THEIR CHRISTMAS TREES

People
are throwing out
    their Christmas trees

We see them
    all along Lake Shore Drive
        bundled up
        trashed
        dumped
            waiting for pickup

Here at home   a tall double balsam
        we cut in the north woods
      and watered   two
        or three times a day
   and inadvertently
      played   in its hearing
proclamations in stereo
    and six part harmony—
        "First comes Christmas, then
           comes spring!" –   has
in a patch of weak sunlight
    put out pussy paws

    All over the tree
      packets of new needles open
Each branch brightens with new green

Such a tree cannot
                be thrown   into a snowbank

If it lasts until February
                from its branches
        we'll hang
                        small
                        red
                        hearts.

ICICLES AND APPLES

We pack our Christmas ornaments away.
Gilt dogs and painted dolls, glass icicles
and wooden apples crowd our festive tray.

Each year I'm sad. "The tree's too dry," you say
and hand me seven bells knit of red wool.
We pack our Christmas ornaments away.

You next take down six feathered birds. Blue jay,
white dove, owl, goldfinch, partridge, cardinal
and wooden apples crowd our festive tray.

Each year, remembering our holidays
in Salzburg, Bruges, Bar Harbor, Istanbul,
we pack our Christmas ornaments away.

A Swedish ram with plaited horns, a clay
teapot, a tiny wire bicycle
and wooden apples crowd our festive tray.

And soon, a unicorn, squirrel, toy-filled sleigh,
a golden heart, a lobster trap with gulls,
and wooden apples crowd our festive tray.
We pack our Christmas ornaments away.

A KARL-THE-ELDER MEDITATION

"... an exercise ... : secure pen or pencil and paper;
unwrap one chocolate Dove heart;
lay it on your tongue, no chewing allowed; write."

Karl Elder

This sad day begins with chocolate
melting on my tongue. I think
of Frost, his poem about the crow:
"and saved some part of a day I had rued."
Will almond chocolate save the day?

The cat howls in the living room.
The melting chocolate breaks in two.
Bobkins knocks from the shelf his
tightly closed can of catnip—he
knows where it is—and when I arrive,

I unscrew the lid to rub catnip
onto the belly of his own little
grey cat. Bobkins tosses his toy
into the air, contented now.
He plays, and I see—really see—the azalea

pink and flourishing under
the light, its blossoms edged
with white, pulsating with quiet life,
thick leaves veined and beautiful.
One small piece of almond still remains.

I chew it thoughtfully, then swallow.

TEMPORARY

This moment
is transient—light glinting
from ice and crystalline drops of melted
snow, snow illuminated by the sun, bright
white, then shadowed and more shadowed,
every branch of evergreen covered
with snow, a world
transformed.

On my desk,
daffodils—opened
as wide as possible—are backlighted
and gleam, yellow in the rich morning light,
dancing, furbelowed, exuberant. On a tree
outside, a red squirrel scatters snow
from every branch he touches.
None of this beauty
will last.

SKIRMISH SONG: TRIUMPHAL MODE

Rain last night beat back the snow.
Patches in the snowfields show
autumn grasses, brown and sere,
lying there this half the year,
flattened long, now spring up, freed:
rain so liberates the weed.

Patches at the base of trees
show snow melts back first from these.
Bands of needles, oak leaves meet.
Everywhere snow's in retreat.
Now we'll see old winter go.
Rain last night beat back the snow.

New Leaves, transparent watercolor and ink

A POET ENTERS THE GOOD YEAR/
LIFE STRIDE 10K

That's me at forty-nine, gasping for air
while running up a hill at my best pace,
for Time is seeded with me in this race.
I run; he flies. Always I feel him there
at my left shoulder, ready soon to pass.
He'll get the inside track near finish line.
Old, wily, full of tricks, he gives no sign
he'll win the race, but always does. Alas.

Officials all deny a real contest:
we race against ourselves for "personal best."
But well I know, I'm in this race for life,
and well I've learned, I'm up against fleet Time.
My personal best won't win this breathless strife . . .
unless I make my feet, in running, rhyme.

THE BIG KAYPRO (THEN)

The big KayPro is the one in my mind,
the one I program at night so
in the morning I have a poem, or the start
of a poem, or lines dancing in my head.
Even though I've had the little KayPro,
the grey one, in its metallic case,
the jeep among computer vehicles,
with its tiny green screen, only
four days, and I've lived with my mind
for life, it's the big KayPro
I don't know. For the little KayPro,
I have a user's guide titled Read Me
First. My WordStar Command Card
shows combinations of letters for scrolling,
saving, filing, finding, and replacing.
But my mind didn't come with its manual.
Experimentation is my only instruction,
a wasteful way to learn. If I program
my mind, the big KayPro, I don't know
input or output, how to turn it on,
or how to turn it off. If I call
up a poem, I don't know how. And I
haven't yet learned how to Remove Block.

EXCUSE

This week I wrote no poetry
and no poem came uncalled to me.
Three times this week my car broke down.
Each time I drove it into town
white steam roiled out beneath the hood
and there I stood,
on street corners in dark and hail and rain.
It was a pain,
I tell you, and took up time, besides.
Though strangers offered rides,
and friends their cars and sympathy,
and Roger's tow truck came three times to me,
sweet poesy didn't. This week I rode the bus,
not winged Pegasus.

TWO POEMS, SMALL AND SIMPLE

1

A poem
makes a start
and goes down
in
a
line.

It's a column
of print
record-
ed
in
time.

2

A little poem
without warning
in a rush

comes

like emotion
spilling over
at a touch.

DECISION

My friends ask me why I write villanelles:
    "What is your purpose? Why this ancient form?
    These are dead ashes that you'll never warm."
        "A poem like this is one that never sells—
        Nonsense of rossignols and philomels."
    "You write just like a sophomore in a dorm!
    You'll soon write poems declaring love's a storm,
    your heart a ship adrift on great sea swells!"

I can't defend myself. It all is true.
    I do like villanelles; they're fun to write.
        But I can see their point: the form is dead.
From now on I'll consider it taboo.
    Submitting, I give up without a fight.
        I'll write Petrarchan sonnets now instead.

Spring Glade, transparent watercolor and ink

THE RETURN

The birds are back, visible everywhere in bare trees,
chevrons flashing scarlet on trilling red-winged
blackbirds, who sing their possession of selected marsh
cattails. It's March, and things are . . .
uncertain. But "Hallooo," cries the sandhill crane, in
its crazy, prehistoric laugh, flying with wide wings,
its body bent like a twig, legs trailing. "Hallooo."
Spring is travelling north, pussy willows like bouquets
in the melting snow, and it's coming on fast.

HARBINGERS

Sunlight this morning
casts shadows on the walls.
They are good shadows—
strong spikey leaves of the amaryllis,
dainty intricacies of the azalea.
The light pours through the leaves
as they flourish, pushing toward the sun,
and in me too, jubilation rises:
It is spring. It is spring!

OF PEACE AND CHILDHOOD
For Marlys Joy Creger, 1937-2017

These sibling memories:
"Mo' pea, Gramma, mo' pea," we said,
and hid under her back porch,
sunlight playing
bright slats over our treasure,
the long thin green-gold of early garden peas.
Or older,
sat on our own front steps,
shopping bags filled with booty between us,
sharing the bounty,
splitting pods with small strong fingers,
tipping over the green canoes,
ripping out by a trick,
a quick flick of our tongues
a row or two, single and straight,
or divided and alternating, of plump paddlers,
little green clones.
Downed helicopter propellers piled up
on either side of us and we felt so fine,
eating those endless sweets of spring,
we knew we would live forever through
fadeproof green June days.
Or in evening, excited to be out after dark,
at the summer band concerts
in our local park, we
sat on a blanket,
peas brought in paper bags and better
than buttered popcorn.

And once, when you were very little,
you thought Christmas carolers
were singing, "Sleep
in Heavenly Peas."

SAVING A LIFE HAS NOTHING TO DO
WITH FORGIVENESS

Just a cat, Bip is jealous, formal, loyal.
He's a white-pawed hero with a quirky
temperament. Bip is brave.
He was showing me one day how when I'd left him
outside for hours on a sunny spring afternoon
while I went to work, I was wrong.
He'd waited until I returned to turn
his back and stalk to the neighbors,
tail held high. In the midst
of this demonstration of my reprehensible
inconsideration for cats, as he
marched with dignity toward due appreciation
and the stone fence of the neighbor's line,
a black dog eight times his size bolted
into our backyard, saw me, and began to bark.
Not wanting this to become a regular event,
I shouted, "Go home," too sharply. That
tough cat shot back across the lawn, forepaws
tucked up like Santa's reindeer, positioned
himself between dog and me, and proudly
puffed himself up to be only four times
smaller. The dog, belatedly observing
a maniac cat, a kamikaze cat, retired,
woofing oafishly and ambling back down
the driveway. Bip stayed to see him gone,
rearranged his neat fur, erected his tail,
and with indifferent dignity again
began his slow stalk to the neighbors,
tail waving like a battle flag held high.

A Summer Day, transparent watercolor

THREE SMALL POEMS FOR SUMMER

Bright lemon lilies

blooming in woods of white birch

recall old homesteads.

❧

From our windows we cannot see the sky,

but we can see reflections of birds

flying on the water.

❧

Tall yellow iris

bloom among the river reeds—

goldfinches at rest.

❧

GREY FOX

The grey fox walked under my window as I watched
and could see her back was black, the fur
interspersed with pure white hairs.
Without the window, I could have touched
her. She was so beautiful! Then, and
when she sat proudly upright in our backyard
protecting her four kits, who romped and played
roughly, adorably, trying to climb pine trees
and managing three feet, grumbling as they tussled
over the red meat the grey fox provided.

One day our plump and pretty, long-furred
little cat got out, streaked beyond our reach,
pranced happily in the undergrowth, and met
the grey fox. "Melisande!" I shouted, hearing
the ruckus in the far corner of the lot and knowing.
"Melisande! This way!" and held the porch door
open. The little cat dashed in, eyes wild
with what she had seen, with what she had
too suddenly understood: that the world
was not hers, that prancing might bring trouble
she could not escape. She never went out again.

Late that afternoon, the grey fox sat
proudly back on her haunches, her black
and white fur glimmering, her paws set
just so, protective, erect and still,
as I watched her, and she watched her kits
at pretend play, grumbling,
roughly tussling over their provided food.

LAKE MICHIGAN VILLANELLE
FOR GINI AND HARVEY

Some longtime friends have come to walk the shore,
a scrap of prose and several poems in hand.
We've done this often enough before.

Today once more we'll watch the seagulls soar
and see bright waves roll in upon white sand.
We longtime friends together walk the shore.

We'll swim in clear blue water, then explore
the beach, scattering sanderlings out of their single
    band.
We've done this often enough before.

Just once we found a turtle, and what's more,
Harvey wrote a poem about it, white sand,
blue sky, and friends who walk along the shore.

The turtle's wise old eyes held ancient lore
of surf and sand. We swam and walked the strand.
We'd done this often enough before.

Older, wiser now, we can't ignore
transitions, surf dividing lake from land.
Old friends who still can walk along the shore,
we've haven't done this nearly enough before.

Autumn Along the Shore, transparent watercolor

CONVERSATION

I'm glad I'm me,
Antler
said.
I love myself, but
what would the boy who sailed walnutshell boats
think of this person, of what
I've become?

STAR POEM FOR ANTLER

Interviewed in his living room, Antler
speaks
more of stars than poetry,
of camping than writing.
Each year he backpacks into wilderness,
setting up basecamps to trek
inward
even further.
He explores inner spaces,
also outer.

Drink lots of water before sleeping,
he advises.
You'll wake to relieve yourself
when stars are brightest.
Wrap yourself in a blanket
to stay up
the rest of the night.

Lately
when he camps, he sleeps
much of the day.
He regrets,
he says, time he's wasted
not watching the stars.
He quotes Emerson, commenting
if stars shone only once
every thousand years, how we'd go out to look at them,
how amazed we'd be,
how adoring.

Antler gestures
toward Orion in plasterwhite ceiling,
recreating the sky
with curved splayed fingers.
His greying beard flares up,
every hair backlighted
in combined illumination of lamplight
and starlight.
Constellations wheel like winter geese
in clamorous array above his head, cascading—
a favorite word—
in his rapturous eyes.

CONCEPTION OF KOETHE, JANUARY 1992

At the top of the stairs, three
flights of stairs, entered from an alley
at the back of the substantial
nineteenth century brick apartment building
gone condo,
the poet sits in a white space with his cat Molly,

hugging himself defensively with folded arms,
lightly, being kind,
smiling faintly and self-reflectively
answering questions I put to him.
His casual clothes and haircut say Harvard, Princeton,
and they speak truth.

He speaks in sentences that are not sentences,
but phrases like ponderous hummingbirds
darting here and there, altering direction
abruptly. As he talks,
imperceptibly the light changes
on his white walls. The afternoon deepens.

His poems have no subjects, he says,
no real subjects—just the passing of time,
the fleeting transience of our subjective
consciousness, what it feels like to be
captive, alive
inside our walls of mind.

Walls reflect walls. His inner space
echoes with that space,
white, airy, insubstantial.

At the top of the old brick apartment building,
turned condo,
is a domed void as large as any in his poems.

It is orderly, pleasing, but abstract.
One walks through this, now and again encountering a
waterglass, a shelf of books, a father's
green Song dynasty horse, a living being.
These are quite specific, but
do not endure. The dominant feeling

is of emptiness, time passing,
the poet speaking in phrases
that don't always connect, communicating
almost perfectly, the isolation almost
all there is, the cat as happy as any other
cat, playing furiously with a red rubber band.

CASUALTY

Published first by Doubleday, he never
has forgotten it. Many rivers,
he says, have gone over that particular dam
since he came home from Nam
and found his poems in print, a war anthology.

Answering questions by interrogating his past,
he notes success didn't last,
the next poems merely small press,
nicely illustrated, those following less
distinguished: self-published, the printing tacky.

Twisted sideways on the sofa, he turns
to point out pots of paperwhites. He's learned,
he says, to force them into early spring.
He'd do the same thing
if he could with poems. His paperwhites are ivory;

their cool fragrance fills the room.
On the table, stacks of spiral notebooks entomb
years of writing practice, endless hours.
Beneath their sweetness, the flowers
emit a secret second odor, unpleasant, funky,

thin, a wisp of smell, their underlying scent.
How did his past dwindle into this present?
Thoughts gnaw at him like rats through rope.
He'd returned from Nam with such incredulous hope,
committing all his life to poetry.

SUSAN

Grieving,

fragile, she speaks of poetry.

Now energy flows

from her, as in those tendrils

the morning glory

shoots forth, that hover over nothing, two feet out,

seeking light and support,

and, finding both,

cling,

twine,

bring forth

buds and burst

into bloom,

blue

and glorious.

PROFESSOR ROSENTHAL IN THE PARK, 1983
For M. L. Rosenthal

As if in a painting by Chagall, the girl
leapt above the grass and kissed you. She
started when she saw you, sped past the morning
bag-ladies and unshaven benchmen taking
showers in the municipal lawn sprinklers,
past the little dogs and obedient
masters on urgent morning errands,
past the policemen on his metropolitan
brown horse surveying the déjeuner
sur l'herbe of hidden wine and whiskey,
past the businessmen stumbling in mid-stride
while adjusting their ties, and the juggler
lifting bowling pins out of his briefcase,
past black women rocking white
babies in strollers, past strollers
enjoying walks across Washington Square,
past the muscular jogger in his loincloth,
the plump joggers in their bunnysuits,
the gaunt joggers in t-shirts, headbands, and Adidas
run down at the heels but patched with shoe goo,
past students clustered about you
talking of poetry, and rose with the flock
of pigeons. Carrying her bouquet upright
in one hand, her blond hair flying backward,
she lifted herself from the grass and settled
a kiss on your startled cheek. You
smiled as if every day in the park
you were surprised by kisses and the muse.

Fallen Leaves, transparent watercolor and ink

MARCHING BAND

I scuffed through bright leaves and October,
November, the months of the marching band.
I was on the inside track, in the gutter
with crisping leaves, point person,
first row. I played piccolo. We
picked up the beat and entered the march;
I danced high above the band in notes.
Following our white majorette, her
tall white hat, we made intricate
maneuvers, rows reversing directions
to march between rows, but I, high
under arching elms, trilled my melody,
in sunlight filtering golden through
leaves more beautiful than stained glass.
Wildly free, I piped, an autumn Pan,
a young revolutionary hearing drums,
piccolo player of Merrill High.

But on Homecoming, our majorette lost
her way, abandoned her route. We kept
our discipline, marching in ranks
down streets where no one applauded,
lost parade playing to children on curbs,
housewives hanging out wash, old men,
raking. We played loudly to keep
our spirits up and marched down hills,
following our majorette's receding
white hat. Above the band I piped,
wildly free, marching in formation,
piccolo player in the lost parade,
eagerly schooling myself for life.

AFTER WASHING WINDOWS
I HAVE MY REWARD

Not only
have I been outside
from earliest hours watching
smudged panes
disappear under circling fingers
and looked up from resting
clean windows
against maple trees
to see
a cardinal
singing among scarlet leaves

but also
when I carry the clear windows
balancing their frames carefully on my hips
I hold between my hands
mirrors of reflected trees
and sky
and when I
wheel
slowly
arms outstretched to this dancing partner
the duplicated world
whirls
around me
and I feel
so free
almost weightless
as I did once playing statues
as a child.

LAKE MICHIGAN SHORE

All summer there were stars.
But in October,
lake effect took over.
Black night followed grey day.
For three months we went without seeing
even
the moon.

ONIONS

Onions the color of autumn beech
leaves rest on our table within easy reach,
smooth, shaped like hens'
eggs, except for two growing ends,
remnants of root and stalk.
You sit mute, while I talk,
both braiding ropes of onion, easy labor.
Their skins are glossy, texture of paper,
perhaps of beech leaves just beginning to dry.
"Almost finished," I
tell you, counting out loud to twenty-eight.
One feels good as a worry stone, a weight
for the palm, a fit size for hefting.
I watch your fingers deftly
braid and wonder how you now twist everything.
Dirt still clings
to some, stalks broken off, dried to a peak.
Left on the table, beak to beak,
they're small quails, resting on darkened under-
bellies. What you refuse to say could rend
my heart. One on my palm, turned over,
shows root end
like a sunflower's center, brown-black,
then almond skin darkened to umber
and a break where paper folds back
outgrown like snakeskin,
then a smoothness ribbed in
pearl, then an emerging freshness, cream
striped in the faintest, mildest green.

LATE OCTOBER
"Bare ruined choirs, where late the sweet birds sang."
Shakespeare

This morning out our windows, the birches are bare,
and sand castles on the beach are ruined
by pounding waves. The summer birds, those choirs
gathered on slack telephone wires are gone, where-
as we remain, watching the morning light come late
and later, the dusk fall early. How will we endure—the
knowledge of coming cold already in our bones, sweet
memories of summer days become like flown birds
in our receding past, like songs we never sang.

OUT OF THE DARK AND THE PAST

Two-legged only
 seen head-on

 and
 measured by the beam of my brights
 you were too tall
 too stately   unreal
 mere momentary apparition with outspread ears

 Then you leapt
 I swerved
driving sixty-five
 into the dark   seeing
 you twist in the air and my headlights
 to hurtle
 diagonally backward
 to live
 to land   miraculously
 Mummer
 from England's most ancient time
 behind your launching place
 shadowy
antlered acrobat

NOVEMBER 31, 1991: 4:20 A.M.

Sleepless at night, I
wander through the house in company
of small dim lights nonexistent
ten years ago.
Suddenly they were there, like the magician's
illuminated mice
mostly at floor level.
The digital clock now reads
4:23:37
in ice blue numbers
silently clicking away seconds,
minutes of our sleep
and wakefulness.
Orange-red switches on surge protectors
glow warmly.
I wander between them in the dark
as if drifting between lighthouse beams,
only furniture of a shipwrecked night.
Round orange nightlights
radiate security in the bathroom,
on the stairs,
and the answering machine's red button
is small and bright on the telephone table.
Our neighbor's spot, one block away,
floods the kitchen window like
the moon, and looking out
my study window
I see a single star.

HE POLISHED HIS MOTHER'S SILVER
LAST NIGHT

"Look at this, then look at this,"
he said, placing
tarnished ladle and transformed spoon
side by side.
"Even the scratches are gone."
Proud of his work, he picked up the ladle,
poured silver polish into its thin worn bowl,
rubbed with flannel rags,
and began
taking the old tarnish back,
making his hands and soft cloth
black with it, to recover
that silver.
Soon the ladle was smooth.
It gleamed like childhood, a subdued light.
His mother newly gone,
he was bringing her back, polishing his past,
recreating in hands and memory
meals she had made,
Monday, Tuesday, with such regularity,
warmth and mashed potatoes served up
in that silver spoon, comfort and good soup
served up in that ladle.
He was smoothing out scratches,
rubbing out lines
age had made
on old silver
and his dead mother's face.

The Peninsula in Winter, transparent watercolor

DEER IN DECEMBER

Silent as tree stumps,
deer are bedded down in our backyard.
Rounded warm bodies
brown as beech leaves after November,
December rains,
ears alert, slightly back even at rest,
they are gentle, vulnerable,
obviously meant for grasses and corn,
mild animals come to the feast
this December day
and staying for sleep.

Or perhaps warmth?
Wind blows hard at the treetops;
a blizzard's predicted.
The great lake roars.

One deer looks up, turning her head.
Fine white hairs line her soft ears.
Too close, I see deer resemble camels,
knees and joints
all cobbled together,
lying down so difficult
they must carefully kneel, one leg,
the other,
snapping their necks back
with an awkward jolt
to fold their hind legs under them.

I think of hummingbirds momentarily
still,
our greater pleasure in their flight.

I remember deer
shimmering in and out of moonlight,
silently gliding into deep woods,
elusive as unicorns,
beauty glimpsed as fleetingly
as first snowflakes in winter
melting as they fall.

LOVE SONG FOR A MOTHER-IN-LAW

My mother-in-law's eyes are hidden by
thick glasses. She's short. She wears a red
fur-collared coat—a gift from Dad, long dead.
Behind the lenses, one eye's blind; one eye,
still "good," is teased by cataract. She's short
of breath, now fears both stairs and curbs, needs help
and hates it. Years ago, with this young whelp
and that already grown, we strode athwart
night sidewalks, empty avenues, in dark
Manhattan's after hours. In Central Park,
we glimpsed December stars. We flanked her, small
and seasonal in her red coat, four sons—all
protective, tall—a daughter, husband, wives.
Invincible, we linked our arms and lives.

THIS MORNING

The crows of December
visit our bird feeder,
shiny black, resplendent
in feathers, thick-
necked, elegant, large,
with raucous caws.
Twa courbies, but without
that reputation,
without applause,
simply themselves,
beautiful
in the pale winter sunlight.

NEIGHBOR

Inadvertently,
I have upset a squirrel
outside my study window.

Now he folds his paws
over his belly,
chirring at me through the glass.
His small body cannot contain such fury.
He quivers, shadow tail shaking with rage.

Argumentatively
hanging upside down on the maple,
legs braced and ready for anything,
he lashes his tail,
scolding.

Supple indicator of mood,
the tail curls and uncurls his anger,
question mark, exclamation, question mark,
exclamation, punctuating
his vehement chatter,
signaling
his grave displeasure, indignation,
and worse.

NIGHT DREAM: BACK FROM THE STYX

She grabbed my hand and pressed it.
"You have my box," she said.
That was not true. She had *my* box:
an old hat, leather gloves I never wore
anymore, a fake flower corsage bunched
up into a mess of yellow stamens, pink petals.
I'd pulled her out of my car, an old
woman, not knowing where she was going,
she'd scrambled in. So had others,
a wayward lot, crawling over the back bumper
and into the back seat crowded with boxes
loosely packed and thrown in for travelling.
The official looked at me, at her.
I was in the wrong line, I shouldn't
have been there at all. "This line goes
through, does it?" I asked, "And that
goes to the water?" "No," he answered,
his body stiff. "This is the line
for the ferry." It was dark in there;
people were lost. I was in the wrong line
and would need to turn around the damp
concrete abutments. Where was I going,
with my boxes, my old belongings?
I don't know. And I don't know anything
more about my old companion, the woman
who'd gotten into my car. When I drove off,
she and the others rode in the seat behind me.

COMING TO TERMS

This morning I am learning German.
My tongue cups the words and my throat
     opens for the gutterals
My voice takes pleasure

                          Always
    these words have been in shadows

                             dark
     with unexpressed meaning
These words for years have hung around
    the edges of my life
              shy thugs
     scuffing their shoes in the background
    preferring anonymity   faceless
      behind their masks
Now I see them
    and confront them openly
I speak

Language of the enemy   outlawed
                     words
   shouted in newsreels by
     stiff-armed marching men
   spoken in filmed prisons by
     uniformed men   who meant harm
                  unspoken
language of my grandmother
   late in life I learn your rhythms
     Guten Morgen
     Herr Wagner

A child   I heard German
when Grandmother
wound my skein of yarn   counting
       eye . . .nz
           sv . . . eye
                dr . . . eye
                     f . . .eer   magic
numbers I recounted to myself
    growing up
        grandmother gone
                    counting
as I skipped through the years
    fumf
        zex
             zee . . . ben   skip rope
flying
feet dancing   growing up
    ah . . .kt
        n . . . oin.
            tzain   with silent
numbers on my tongue

IN MY LIFETIME

There's no escaping it.
This happened in my lifetime:
the rise of Hitler,
the building of concentration camps,
the Gulag,
the crushing of Central Europe.
Thirty-five living people pushed
into an underground cell
with insufficient air.
And that was only Europe,
not to mention Asia
and Africa.
This happened in my lifetime,
while I heard the wind in the pines
and listened to loons
calling at one end of the lake
and to wolves answering and echoing
at the other.

JUDY: JANUARY 2, 1984

I learned on Friday how you are to die.
Your sentence: months. One month to four.
Not years, as you deserve.
But who among us doesn't lie
With that "deserve"? We don't "deserve"
to live. It's not our wages, pay for trust.
Instead: a gift. And when we open gifts,
dark packages all brightly wrapped,
their bows and papers glittering, we must
say thanks. We do not beg for more,
unmannerly, whatever we might think.
Gift horses, mouths, we say,
and so on. And give thanks.
We two had got sabbaticals. You said,
"We've worked our bloody asses off. Hey, we
deserve it!" Odd,
you'll never write your novel now.
You'll spend your paid free time on being dead.
And this bright life now glittering in snow,
cut iris on your desk now cupping light to lift
toward a forgotten sky—see
the wrapping may be all there is.
The gift when wrapped is beautiful: hang on to this
as you begin to burrow into pain.
If he's around, say thanks to God.

SONNET

I'd like to have a manuscript to work on.
I need something to do this morning. Now
the tulips on the desk are open. Snow
outside the window rumples. Blue jays lurk in
spruces, bob their cry, then fly for seed
put out to save them. So, could I save you
this winter morning, I would put out all
I own. Out would go my tulips, shawl,
chairs, desk, rug, crates of books, two lamps, my new
blue blotter, stuff no deer or blue jays need,
surprised to see drifts spill over a rug
and swirl round chairs. No rug will tamp down chill,
no shawl ward off cold death for one so ill,
nor tulips warm the grave soon to be dug.

RUMINATIONS ON DEATH (NOW)

1

That doesn't mean there isn't confetti
in these poems—see! There's a handful
thrown upward and now falling: gold, blue, scarlet
—and streamers of wind pushing clouds
across the cobalt sky. And birds: nuthatches,
cardinals, a great blue heron in flight,
wings outstretched and flapping slowly, its long
neck crooked like undersink plumbing. See! The
yellow-breasted tit with its black stripes and the
amiable chickadees. This poem on death is
full of these beautiful, airy, flying things. This
poem on death is filled with joy.

2

What does death do, but remind us to live?
Death will take care of death. We don't
have to practice to get good at it. It will
happen, by itself. And we, meanwhile,
get to live each moment, get to fill
each minute with wonder, awe,
love, gratitude, joy, and boundless energy.

I'M WRITING THIS POEM BECAUSE

the girl clambered so quickly
from the bubbling spa and splashed
into other water. She was small
and thin and it was a moment in
my life as she landed feet first
in the pool, so fast, heels flashing.

Just then the woman in a black bathing
suit, standing at the edge of the pool,
turned and walked along the rim and
through a few seconds of her own thirtieth
year, dangling from her fingers
a pair of green swimming goggles.

ALMOST

Almost, I'm beginning to get it: that the wind
ruffling the leaves is the same breath in the boy
swimming, the breath blown out in bubbles
as he dives underwater, and the same breath in me,
as the wind moves through the swaying trees.

Looking Forward, transparent watercolor

SUPERMUSE WILL HELP THE OLD WOMAN OF THE CRANBERRY BOGS FIND HER VOICE

Silently, the old woman follows deer trails,
    heel-toe, heel-toe, walking the way
        Menomonee once walked in these woods,
        moccasined feet making no sound.

She stands motionless for an hour or more
    watching deer browse in front of her,
    remaining still when they confront her
        and stamp delicate hooves in challenge
        and inquiry,
    making no sound until,
        assuring themselves she
            has turned into a tree, become
            rooted,
        in bewilderment and calm
        they begin again to nibble the soft grass.

She stops to watch red squirrel and chipmunk,
    and the high squeaking sound that comes
        from her pursed lips
        placed against the back of her hand
    is the voice of the chipmunk,
        who stops to listen.

She whistles to the birds
    with their own loose looping whistle
        followed by two falling notes,
    and brings bright orioles down from birches,
        in a flutter of black and orange wings.

When she walks on sand, barefoot along the shore,
      she hears the voice of the sea
          but cannot answer.

With humans, too, she is silent.

Now Supermuse will give her words, human
      phrases that nonetheless will fit her mouth.
She will be able to use words to name the chipmunk
    and to define her universe, to set things in motion
      and to say who she is.

Supermuse will give the old woman
      of the cranberry bogs
              words
    and the old woman will be grateful.

SUPERMUSE VISITS THE LIVE POETS' SOCIETY

Supermuse stands by, guarding manuscripts and guitar
            while the poets load their canoe
                    with blankets and food,
                    towels and life preservers.
When they launch the canoe, Supermuse steps in
                and takes her place in the center.
        She dangles her fingers languidly
                in the warm water
                        as they paddle out
                                beneath the blue dome
                                of the sky,
    and she laughs with delight when they turn the canoe
                toward wide horizontals
                            of blue lake,
                    green marsh and distant shore.

As they drift through fields of waterlilies—
                white chalices opening to the sky,
                round yellow fists closed lightly over
                            maroon interiors—
            she is the first to see mute swans,
                        two adults and three cygnets,
                swimming toward them
                        through a channel of reeds.
When the male swan swims close, and silently
                        at eye level
                confronts each of the poets in turn
        Supermuse remains still, respectfully motionless,
                until he swims aside
                        and allows them to pass.

She watches two white cygnets and a downy gray
                preen themselves,
                                their necks and bills
                now awkward in these new motions.
She admires their mother as the five swans
                                in ranked order
                swim back
                through the reed channel,
        poets following,
                paddling so softly
                                the only sounds
        are trills from red-winged blackbirds
                clinging sideways to reeds
                and the regular
                        low *gloock*
                                of the frogs.

As the poets leave reeds behind and enter the lake,
                Supermuse dreams
                                among clouds drifting
                                        in still water.
        Observing reflected goldfinches
                                in undulating flight,
                she directs the poets to follow them
                        and pull their canoe up
                                        onto the furthest shore.
When, paddling leisurely, they near that curve of land,
                Supermuse points to a sandhill crane
                                        rising,
                        ruddy outstretched wings
                                six feet across.

The poets disembark under an oak tree,
              spread their blankets on the grass,
              swim, eat,
                  and exclaim over the outstretched arms
                       of other ancient oaks
                            on a nearby hill.
Then they sing their poems to each other,
          and Supermuse listens intently,
              smiles,
                  and approves.

RAMBLING

Supermuse keeps pace with the old woman
                    of the cranberry bogs.

Avoiding poison ivy, she rambles
            through a field of purple gayfeather
        and sits down in the hot sun to listen to waves.

She sees red squirrels clambering up trunks of jack pine
        and follows the trail of deer
            to watch them browse.

She forages with the old woman
                for thimble-sized blackberries,
        looking under their reddened September leaves
            and avoiding the thorns.

In that season of the year when green birch leaves
                    hold yellow
                just beneath their surface
            and hillsides are brilliant with goldenrod
                and yellowing leaves
                        of milkweed
            and ladybugs and monarch butterflies
                    gather on beaches,
                turning driftwood orange,
        Supermuse walks with the old woman
                    under the full blue sky,
            hears cicadas hum, and
            gathers hot sun
                to her shoulders and arms,
        senses it on the backs of her legs.

She walks knee-deep in tousled waves
                    tumbling toward shore
        and kneads firm sand ridges beneath her toes.

She looks at rounded stones
                    under sun-ripples of clear water
        and feels joy!
                    and smiles at the old woman
                                of the cranberry bogs
                    and is kind to her.

❧☙❧☙❧☙❧☙❧☙❧☙

ೞ⅃ೞ⅃ೞ⅃ೞ⅃ೞ⅃ೞ⅃ೞ⅃ೞ⅃ೞ⅃ೞ⅃ೞ

ACKNOWLEDGEMENTS

No one does anything alone, especially when one is scarcely aware of doing it. Looking back, I find, while writing poems mostly for and by myself, I also hesitantly stayed on a tenuous path in poetry—and thus have a surprising number of people met on the way to thank for the arrival of this book.

Among them are Lucille Trantow, English teacher at Merrill High, and professors at the University of Wisconsin-Madison, including Madelaine Doran, and M. L. Rosenthal of NYU and the always amiable X. J. Kennedy.

All the poets I interviewed for *Creativity and the Poetic Mind* helped, including Barbara Helfgott Hyett, who asked why I didn't take my own poetry seriously. There are Karl Gartung and Anne Kingsbury, who founded the remarkable poetry bookstore Woodland Pattern in Milwaukee, where I wandered in one day and stayed to take a workshop, and Louisa Solano at the Grolier in Cambridge, Massachusetts.

Gini Holland, Harvey Taylor, and Noah Dixon of the Live Poets Society were among the very first to see my poems in the 1980's. Karl Elder's group of poets at Mead Library in Sheboygan saw a few of them again, plus some new ones, decades later.

In the 2020-21 year of Covid, Belle Ragins, Erik Thelen, Jim Tobin, Gary Shea, and Steve Rassel gathered weekly for Black River Poetry zooms (BuRP), Sunday nights that sustained us all.

Susan Firer and Gini Holland read over parts of the

manuscript and, being often published themselves, kindly shared their expertise. Wilson Engel offered monumental encouragement and decisive practical assistance. Editor and Publisher Lindsay Fairgrieve was sensitive in her response, notably patient and tremendously efficient in making this book happen. Terry Marks and dear nieces Laura Creger and Kathleen Kennedy Tobin reassuringly stepped up to fix a technical glitch.

Without Gary Shea, the book would have no illustrations, as he generously photographed my watercolors, then over and over again put the photos into proper format.

And, of course, I want to thank Jim Tobin, who always listens to my poems, and who has written some himself.

CRITICALLY

ABOUT THE POET

In addition to poems, Jean Tobin has published articles, reviews, and introductions, as well as two books: *Creativity and the Poetic Mind* (Lang, 2004) and, with Ruth Saxton, *Woolf and Lessing: Breaking the Mold* (St. Martin's, 1994; MacMillan, 1994).

Co-founder of the land trust Glacial Lakes Conservancy, Dr. Tobin is Professor Emerita of English with the University of Wisconsin Colleges. Along with lectures and presenting professional papers nationally, she has given public readings of poems at Woodland Pattern, the poetry bookstore in Milwaukee, and in various towns in Wisconsin.

Dr. Tobin began painting in 2001, had her first show three years later, and has since been in numerous group exhibitions and two-person shows, as well as ten solo shows. She is a member of several watercolor societies and greatly enjoys painting en plein air.

She lives in Black River, a wooded area just south of Sheboygan, Wisconsin, with her husband. Their home has been shared with a succession of cats: Bip and Harlequin, then Melisande and Bob (the sociable Bobkins), and now the fierce and beautiful Melody.

Made in the USA
Monee, IL
06 June 2021